SUPER SULTRY SINSATIONS

BY
AIYSHA SWALLOWGREN

© 2023 Aiysha Swallowgren

All rights reserved. No part of this publication may be reproduced, distributed, or transmitted in any form without the express written permission of the publisher, except in the case of brief quotations embodied in critical reviews and certain other noncommercial uses permitted by copyright law.

ISBN 979-8-9878596-1-2
First Printing April 2023
Printed in United States of America

Contents

Analyze / 5, Athletic / 6, Attention / 7, Baby / 8, Belt / 9, Better / 10, Board / 11, Bored / 12, Breastplay / 13, Buttons / 14, Cane / 15, Caring / 16, Compliment / 17, Creampie / 18, Creature / 19, Customized / 20, Date / 21, Delight / 22, Desired More / 23, Different Kind of Hot / 24, Direct / 25, Direction / 26, Done / 27, Draining / 28, Dripping / 29, Dying / 30, Especially / 31, Explode / 32, Feeding / 33, First / 34, Force / 35, Fox / 36, Goddess / 37, Good / 38, Gym / 39, Handling / 40, Honest / 41, Hot / 42, Impressed / 43, Into / 44, Invading / 45, Irresistible / 46, Lapping / 47, Long / 48, Lord / 49, Love / 50, Lover / 51, Meow / 52, Mermaid / 53, Might / 54, More / 55, More Pleasure / 56, Morning / 57, Naughty / 58, Offend / 59, Oh My / 60, On / 61, Part / 62, Personal / 63, Play / 64, Playfully / 65, Please / 66, Pleasing / 67, Priceless / 68, Professionally / 69, Prove / 70, Punishing / 71, Pussy Suck / 72, Puzzling / 73, Question / 74, Real / 75, Record / 76, Release / 77, Resist / 78, Ripped / 79, Ripping / 80, Romance / 81, Romantic and Nice / 82, Rougher / 83, Sketching / 84, Skirt / 85, Smiling Dose / 86, Snack / 87, So / 88, Sowing / 89, Special / 90, Squeeze / 91, Squirting Doll / 92, Steak / 93, Steaming / 94, Stray / 95, Studying / 96, Taking / 97, Talent / 98, Talking / 99, Taste Drive / 100, Teaching / 101, Team / 102, Thought / 103, Thoughts / 104, Thread / 105, Tomato / 106, Too / 107, Trash / 108, True / 109, Twisted / 110, Very Special / 111, Whole / 112, Write / 113, Yeah Fuck / 114, Younger / 115

Analyze

She asked if I enjoy anal starting to analyze
You first I start smacking your hips and thighs
When I grab your hair the look in your eyes
Beckoning me to destroy your hole the size
Of your hot hole stretches as I analyze
You the harder I hit you, the more I pulverize
Your ass the higher your temperature starts to rise
Your favorite is when I use several zip ties
You're blindfolded and love how I always surprise
Your senses with words that really tantalize
You and I'm in your mind as you love when I analyze

Athletic

She asked if I considered her to be athletic
First off miss you have great genetics
I think your body is the reason I'm poetic
I want you to feel very warm and energetic
When I whisper you're my definition of athletic
You workout very hard and your body is epic
Your eyes are fascinating, and your body electric
You're shockingly tone, I need a medic
If you wear any less clothes you're so magnetic
I'm drawn most to your mind but yes you're athletic

Attention

She asked what she had to do to get my attention
You can lay back and carefully listen
All I can think of is making you glisten
I'm very polite, but I'm certainly no gentleman
I know the best focus of your attention
Imagine my tongue relieving all of your tension
Your hips and your pleasure experience such ascension
When I share with you another naughty invention
Teacher says that you'll have to stay for detention
I'll do things to you that you'll never mention
To anyone else but I create such suspension
I've got you touching yourself, I have your attention

Baby

Hot momma started speaking to me like a baby
Which means I get to show her what a lady
Does to me I'm mash you like a potato and supply the gravy
I know exactly what makes the most savory
Sensations let me feed on you like a baby
Your breast in my mouth so full and weighty
When I think about your top I get so wavy
You make waves of passion has anyone told you lately
That you might very well be the nastiest creature maybe
Ever, you're a filthy fucking slut baby

Belt

She asked how to make her say yes and I took off my belt
She desired discipline her needs were heartfelt
The harder I hit her ass and start to pelt
Her with blows the more it makes her pussy melt
I'm making her say yes, yes, yes with my belt
She wanted to be a brat so I dealt
With her naughtiness by leaving a permanent welt
On her body she would holler and yelp
She loved when I forced her obedience with my belt

Better

She said that she would try to be better
I laughed as she's a trendsetter
I bet she looks amazing in leather
Right now I'm thinking about whether
You could possibly get any better
Perhaps a better question is can you get wetter
Start really rough I know there's a lever
In your body that turns when a man is exceptionally clever
I'm the spiciest, hotter than a ghost pepper
Wait I mean you are inhaling my pecker
You swallowed the whole thing, can't get better

Board

She asked what I feel when we speak I replied board
She looked at me confused like I struck a chord
She got very angry, she was really floored
I looked her in the eye, now I'm very forward
Listen lady I said you make me stiff as a board
She giggles like you had me going, good lord
She was never in the circus but was an expert at swallowing a sword
When she reads my words she wants me to come towards
Her and grab her hair banging her against the headboard
I release all her tension, as all that passion is stored
Right in her lap and I make her feel restored
When it comes to lip service I deserve an award
I watch as she starts licking her juices off the floorboard
This is what I mean when I say you make me stiff as a board

Bored

I would never let her get even close to bored
I took her body in my hands and explored
Her flexibility, her mouth deserves an award
I throw her against the wall and use my sword
To beat her properly, Barbie you'll never be bored
They should put your ass on a billboard
The way I keep ripping your clothes off can't be ignored
I've got a whole lot of aggression stored
Up you're so nasty I'm sure that you've whored
Yourself out if you haven't done it before
I'll put you to work, you love being adored
Like a piece of meat as I sprayed and poured
Myself all over her pretty face giving her reward
How much pain she can take will be explored
She's winking at the camera as I record
Don't worry slut, you're never going to get bored

Breastplay

She very much enjoyed sensational breastplay
She would close her eyes and lay
Back and put her body on full display
She wanted it naughty, she loved the dismay
I caused her body and now her hands start to stray
You're roughly and swiftly starting hot breastplay
She told me to unload, to spray
Her breast and face that's the way
That she cums the hardest her breasts they
Needed attention, she was hungry for great breastplay

Buttons

She asked if I will push all of her buttons
Which made me laugh because there's nothin
I love more than making her start shovin
A finger inside her this is making it start runnin
Down her leg I'm going to push all your buttons
You're going to make yourself sore from all the rubbin
You're rubbing yourself as you remember cummin
Lightning bolts and waves of pleasure as you are shudderin
She enjoys my intense and unique lovin
As I use her hands to carefully start smotherin
Her in her juices taste your secretions you're sluttin
It up so much I'm pushing all your buttons

Cane

I broke my ruler over her ass so I grabbed my cane
I hit her so hard it made her brain
Stop thinking of nothing but the hot pain
She said I'm fucking sorry sire let me explain
I hit her tits and it made her exclaim
Take me sir I am yours please claim
Your hot holes most men are soft and lame
You sir are a most flexible and brutal wooden cane
After I'm done her body will never be the same
I shoved it repeatedly in her tight ass when I came
I hit her repeatedly on her back with my cane

Caring

She has needs and with skill I start caring
For them she spreads her legs and is glaring
At me saying it's not going to lick itself stop staring
I'm licking her through what she's wearing
Excellent lip service made her forget sand stop caring
I'm using my tongue to make her start swearing
Most men aren't comfortable baring
Their hearts openly with her I'm daring
I'm daring her imagine me strongly tearing
Her dress she enjoys when I stop caring
Who's watching she's so ready she is raring
To go I'm her plumber and I'm here to start repairing
Her pipes are leaking and I'm hotly declaring
I love your wide, beautiful body your childbearing
Hips are like a work of art I'm comparing
Her to art and being deliciously caring

Compliment

It was like air to her, a sincere compliment
Was the best way to make her senses sprint
She needed things so nasty she didn't hint
She just opened her legs and bent
Over making me pitch a tent
I smacked her hard, leaving an imprint
Rough treatment was her favorite compliment
I'm refreshing to her soul, like a peppermint
I took her further tan anyone ever went
Before my style unique as a fingerprint
Making things uniquely was the highest compliment

CREAMPIE

She wanted to be totally full so she begged for a creampie
As I thrust into her like a hammer I said let's try
Something covering her mouth now why
Don't you ever learn your lesson, you will comply
With my directions can't speak so no reply
I'll make you go out in public with a hot creampie
Leaking down your legs and reaching your thigh high
Socks you suck on your thumb and give me the eye
I know how to make you really start to sigh
My words are putting an end to those dry
Lips I'm singing you a really nasty lullaby
About the filthy urges you want me to satisfy
Stick it in my ass please sir, she begs for another hot creampie

CREATURE

You are such a pretty little creature
I don't believe I've ever met someone so impure
You're dressed as a nun, hot for preacher
You sit on the dryer and I'm either
Going to explode now or later naughty creature
You're a fascinating sexbomb, you're the main feature
I'm watering your garden and I'm sure
That your flesh desires the naughtiest teacher
You're leaking everywhere, what a delicious creature

Customized

It was flattering to her when I carefully customized
Something especially for her it was wise
To put her needs first it made her thighs
Very warm, it made her overflow I capsized
Her vessel my making something hotly customized
Being worshipped made her feel so prized
The effect of my words really surprised
Her body the effect of polite and civilized
Admiration that cared only about how best to emphasize
That she's desired, definitely worth the effort to make customized
Then I showed her how my muscular tongue fertilized
Her garden the more she drips the more I utilize
It made her incredibly hot to be idolized
How best to turn her on by doing it customized
You make my body feel so energized
Truly dear, you have such beautiful and captivating eyes

Date

She asked where I'd tale her if we went on a date
I told her get dressed fancy, we are going to Cheesecake
Factory and I don't know if you enjoy steak
But all I can think about is dessert, that cake
All I will focus on is how to make you shake
I want you shaking with anticipation on our date
I want you dreaming of me when you wake
Up as you continue to remain still as I slowly rake
My hands over your body making you feel so awake
I awaken your senses and there is no mistake
In the restaurant you gave me a unique keepsake
Your damp panties as you whispered you really make
Me so hot, I've never gotten this hot on a date

Delight

I like making your day better and giving you delight
You're the kind of woman that enjoys dynamite
Conversation, the effect on your body as it starts to excite
Sweet words are best wrapped with polite
Admiration, you are my ultimate delight
There's so many things to admire you're very bright
You brighten my world with the way you ignite
My creativity there's so many things to highlight
About you especially what you do to my appetite
You're such a stunning creature, you are quite
Unique and bring my world endless delight

Desired More

She said she felt more desired or desired more
Her brain is my most favorite place to explore
The more I whisper, the more she craves an encore
I'm very sweet, unless she wants it hardcore
I tease her slowly until she desired more
Being desirable was something that made her roar
With passion being so inspiring makes her spirits soar
The more I write to her the more sore
Her wrist gets I said you're doing it again, touching your
Hottest spots there's something spicy about how I adore
Your whole being, it makes me feel such stored
Passions, you truly couldn't be desired more

Different Kind of Hot

She really enjoyed elaboration on a different kind of hot
She loved being taken and now she's caught
In between my hands her neck got
Very heated I was making her a different kind of hot
I had her ride me and she was happy to squat
On top of me as her red face really fought
For air even right now just the thought
Of her choking makes her explode like buckshot
In her chest she's breathing barely, not a lot
She's drooling and gagging I smear her snot
All over her face she's crying her eyes bloodshot
I put her in her place, it's her favorite spot
Being destroyed gets her a different kind of hot

Direct

She wanted me to be very explicit and direct
I want you to imagine that as you slept
You are tied up and gagged so you won't expect
To be treated like a piece of meat, an object
Imagine my strong hands around your neck
I want you to submit, I will direct
You like how I do things you'd never expect
Being a tied up good girl got her so wet
You're on your knees waiting to accept
Your punishment as my feet stepped
On your face is that finally direct
Enough for you as you're prettiest when you've wept
I'm turned on by your fascinating intellect
My words get you hot I'm able to affect
Your body expose it now for me to inspect
Be my nasty, needy, filthy fucking bucket
You're turned on by me being so direct

Direction

She likes there this was heading, a different direction
Someone that focused on her mind and midsection
When I whisper that she's a beautiful expression
Of art I say that you are a glorious reflection
Sincere admiration is a tantalizing direction
Most men only care about getting their erection
Taken care of but I've found such perfection
In making you heated in all your sensitive sections
I'm in your lap, lapping it up, no objection
I'm altering your mood, changing your perception
Playfully and hotly do you enjoy this direction?

Done

She asked how I do it, how is it done
I think of you, who's hotter than the sun
Then I think of how much fun
It would be to shock you and stun
You and most importantly how best to make you cum
I imagine when I write you spank your bum
I like thinking of your top becoming undone
As you spread your legs whispering look what you've done
I'd like to be the reason you stick one
Finger in your mouth and taste yourself that's some
Very motivating words have I done
Well am I making it drip and start to run
Down your legs is it super sexy awesome?

Draining

She loves one thing above all else that's draining
My balls she's on her knees and I'm training
Her to take it all ignoring her tears as she's straining
She loves being my receptacle, she is never complaining
She says I'm your filthy bucket and keeps draining
My essence catching every drop and maintaining
Eye contact her hunger for me is entertaining
I'm making her face look like a Jason Pollock painting
Her hands are tied, it gets her so hot when I'm restraining
Her now carefully I'm getting the camera and aiming
It at her like Bill Clinton I'm staining
Her dress it's your fault slut, I'm blaming
You for getting close to be and claiming
That you wanted to drain my balls, get draining

Dripping

I've got her so needy and she's dripping
Down her leg imagining me strongly whipping
Her ass the harder that I start hitting
Her ass the more it makes her insides start splitting
Being used like a dumpster got her dripping
My large legs start repeatedly kicking
Her little body and now she understands listening
I'm going to wipe that smile off your face you won't be grinning
Much longer as I continue roughly dipping
Myself in your hot holes in your face I'm spitting
I'm treating you like garbage and twisting
Your nipples as it makes you really start dripping

Dying

She asked are you going to kill me with pleasure I'm dying
I laughed out loud and whispered I'm frying
Your senses and your brain starts lying
Back and put a finger inside you're trying
Your best to orgasm to death you're dying
For more wetness your pussy is crying
Out from exhaustion I've been electrifying
It all day you find my words most satisfying
As I grab your throat it helps with intensifying
Your pleasure which my hands keep amplifying
You're barely alive, I'd fuck you with my undying
Love and by love I mean that I'm striking
You so hard you'll feel ike your dying

Especially

She asked if I would write something especially
For her imagine my touch light and feathery
Running along your body making your heavenly
Gates open and your legs start shaking readily
I'm in tune with your needs especially
For your desire to experience freshly
Written things I'm watering your roses covering every
Inch with moisture until your hips move desperately
You need a strong firm tongue leaving you breathlessly
If I'm writing something unique I say embrace destiny
Embrace yourself and the juices run especially
Fast when a man is creative and readily
Makes you warm is that what you're feeling presently

Explode

I woke up to her beginning to explode
On my face, she had apparently rode
Me while I was sleeping as I watch my load
Darin out of her as she begged me to unload
Again on her face she yelled please explode
On me and soon her face totally glowed
She knows what to do as I slowed
Down my pace and made her river flow
When it came to cunnilingus I showed
Exceptional talent as my tongue starts to erode
Her inhibitions as I continued to reload
I felt her cover me again, love making her explode

Feeding

She asked for me to fill her, to start feeding
Her hot holes she's begging and pleading
I give her a swift kick and start firmly beating
Her hot ass choking her as she enjoys to struggle breathing
She's so trashy my little dumpster I'm feeding
Her more and more cum which causes overheating
She starts grabbing herself as she's reading
My filthy love note bitch let's get breeding
I'm cumming deep inside her my seeding
Her damp hole now it starts leaking
Down her leg with my finger I am leading
Her to taste herself, eat yourself you're feeding
My depravity now you're bruised and bleeding
It makes her smile, she's totally beaming
From joy as I lick her tears her weeping
Turns me on the nastier I keep treating
Her as my toes go in her hole she starts squeaking
Lick yourself off my foot slut, get feeding

First

She really wanted to know what I'd do first
Starting with hard spanks, you're truly the worst
You're so full of juices I'll make you burst
Beating you, taking you roughly creates thirst
I'm going to make you drink your juices first
You love when I take what I want I never coerce
You I just hove you in my lap headfirst
I'm taking my aggression out, I dispersed
My blows and it makes your body have wild outbursts
I hit my doll until she wildly squirts
I treat her like a toy and she loves when it hurts
You're going to say I'm nothing but a hole first

Force

She likes the way that I could really force
Her to touch herself hotly, of course
She's reading this imagining how I will enforce
My will on her slapping her ass like a racehorse
She loves when I spank her very hard, the force
I use makes her so desperate for intercourse
She loves when I'm extra naughty and get worse
She wants it in the worst way another verse
About her doing what it takes to be head nurse
She walks around with a vibrator in her purse
She hands me the remote so I can coerce
Her to cum in public she loves when I strongly force

Fox

She's super foxy, my little foxy fox
She walks into the gym and everyone gawks
She's wearing a very revealing top it stops
Nobody from enjoying her body, which rocks
You've got sensational cleavage little foxy fox
I wish you'd do jumping jacks then squats
When you walk down the street traffic stops
Do you ever work out in super cute socks
I'm watching you workout, watching while you box
You're hitting things and the way you move your hotbox
Makes me overheat is incredibly sexy hot foxy fox

Goddess

She said the way she inspires me makes her feel like a goddess
I look at her like the sun, she's the hottest
If I only had one chance, one guess
I would bet she loves when I make her a hot mess
I'm teasing her over her clothing, slow to undress
Which lets her know this morning she's a goddess
I'm her favorite way to play and relieve stress
Within me you bring out the very best
I'm your beautiful reflection so I start to address
Your needs and desires for an end to dryness
You want the real good, first class, highness
Service with a smile, use my tongue, being honest
My favorite place is in the lap of a goddess

Good

She needed hot romance, something really good
Nothing gets her hotter than being understood
I'm creating a spark in her lap of firewood
Reminding her of her fleshy needs her womanhood
Needs servicing often and my tongue is quite good
I use my strong hands, embracing her with my manhood
When it comes to exciting her there's a high likelihood
That she's going to wake up the whole neighborhood
When I start giving it to her really good

Gym

I dreamed I ran into her at the gym
She walked by and I couldn't help looking again
So tone, so fit, so curvy yet thin
I don't know what to do when
She starts doing squats at the gym
I love her in bikinis it makes my insides swim
She's got such beautiful hair and a stunning grin
She's so shy and proper, full to the brim
With desires love watching her stretch her limbs
She should be proud of how hot and trim
She is embrace your passions deep within
Think of me watching you while you're at the gym

Handling

She needed a massage badly so I started handling
Her tense body slowly it started happening
Tasty tingling that came from perfect balancing
Of firm with precision she enjoys smooth handling
She starts feeling herself dampening
The tension started leaving as my hands are traveling
Lower her gasping and groaning she's unraveling
I maintain my focus on her body and she's challenging
Me to give it to her with my mouth I'm sampling
Her soft skin and like am artist I'm canvassing
Her body and all negativity is cancelling
I make her sparkle, her face is dazzling
Which happens when she receives excellent handling

Honest

There is something very sexy about being totally honest
Treating you like the nastiest, sluttiest goddess
When I dream it's of how to make you the hottest
I dream of making it too sexy to resist
I want you dripping with desire, being honest
There's one thing to you always promised
That's to do my best, being most honest

Hot

Those pants you are wearing are super hot
I can't believe you cut out that whole spot
Your hole is on display fully I got
Instantly hard when I saw that you forgot
Panties you are displaying it so hot
When I see you on full display my first thought
Is I wonder how much you enjoy getting caught
So exposed and by how you're doing it I think a lot
You are just too sexy, such a sizzling, naughty shot
Your nipples are excited that fought
For attention if excitement is what you sought
Then let me say that you really taught
Me a lesson in being sexy, that is really hot

Impressed

The way I speak to you leaves you impressed
All the hot things that I have expressed
I want to bring this out of you, your very best
You start teasing and rubbing your chest
Your hand desires for it to be pressed
Against the floor being taken like that impressed
You a lot when I relax the parts of you stressed
Exceeding your expectations I suggest
You start rubbing yourself with zest
You are first prize to any beauty contest
Be my naughty nurse and release all unexpressed
Desires with your mouth, show me you're impressed

INTO

I suggested something to her and she said she's not into
That I laughed inside that's exactly why I want you
To do it remind yourself there are few
Things you won't do for money I'm into
Making you do things that really screw
With your mind the very first clue
About who you are and what you are is true
Filth there's only one type of slut that I'm into
That's the kind that does what she doesn't want to do
Collect your juices and use them as glue
For your eyelashes also use it for shampoo
I want you to cover yourself in cum over your tattoos
You desire to get into trouble, that what you are into

Invading

As I whispered you feel me slowly invading
All your senses and you said this is making
Me absolutely dripping and your body starts shaking
You dream of a man that is able to start waking
Up your darkest desires I'm in your mind invading
Imagine I'm grabbing your hair and spanking
You giving you pleasure puddles that I'm creating
I want you rubbing yourself until it's aching
I've got you right on the edge and I'm taking
You beyond pleasure whispering you're breathtaking
I hear you moan and see the desires start escaping
Down your leg the effect of my words is fascinating
You need it badly and I'm breaking
In like a thief, deliciously and hotly invading

Irresistible

She asked if anything could be more irresistible
Than how I make her want to get biblical
Dressed like a nurse ready to get clinical
I throw her easily, she loves how physical
I am with her being tossed was irresistible
To her, I repeatedly take her to the pinnacle
Of pleasures without any touch, with invisible
Mysterious power I do things so inexplicable
It's always freshest with me, always original
I'm your forbidden fruit, totally irresistible

Lapping

She was really enjoying my attention as I kept lapping
Up her desires what started happening
As I focused on how to keep adding
To her pleasure, she started jabbing
Her fingers inside she can't stop grabbing
Herself when she imagines me lapping
Up all of her juices as my lips start smacking
She pushes her ass back she's backing
Up into my face and warmly basking
In my worship I'm always racking
My brain to keep her breathing heavy and gasping
Imagine me slowly and sweetly lapping

Long

She was finding new desires, it's been so long
Since she had something totally soak her thong
She wanted it badly and the more wrong
It was the happier she was to play along
She was hungry for it, it's been too long
Since anyone wrote or sung her a song
On her knees is where she belongs
Being handled by a big man with strong
Hands the pleasure is immensely headstrong
She needs super stimulation, it's been so long

Lord

She said I hear and will obey you lord
I unleashed her wildness so much stored
Aggression I love when she comes toward
Me crawling on her knees let me serve you lord
I'm her large hammer and she's floored
About getting nailed hard I use my sword
To give her a true naughty slut award
She loves sucking out her hot reward
She serves my needs and if I'm ignored
I handcuff her to the metal headboard
She's drowning in my cum, going overboard
Worshipping the body of her powerful lord

Love

She messaged me saying I love
You and it made me want to fully shove
Her face into the ground she starts to rub
Her hot holes pinching her nipples thinking of
Me forcing her on her knees I stand above
Her smacking her face this is what you love
It makes her leak so much there's a flood
Off her juices from sticking it in her rosebud
When I throw her she lands with a hard thud
I'm leaving bruises, a few scars, clean up the blood
I've got much more to show you about love

Lover

I am most definitely a milf toe lover
The wetness leaking out makes another
Thought you sure are a hot motherfucker
You fuck yourself in public not bothering to cover
Just letting your juices leak I want you to smother
Me, I am worshipping in her lap I'm a milf toe lover
The way you show off there's no other
Way to put it I want to use my tongue on you under
The trees hiking hotly in your ass no rubber
I want your explosions in my face let me uncover
Drenched milf toe using my tongue, I'll butter
Your biscuit eating you for breakfast my hunger
Is growing for leaking milf toe, lover

Meow

I'm taking my wildcat into the shower meow
She's pressing her big ass against the glass how
I am going to smack it like this, pow
Feeding her my meat for her kitty chow
My little kitten loves when I touch her meow
I'm watching her drip, drip, drip right now
She's glistening making it easier to plow
Her roughly she's getting so wet wow
Bending her in new ways she's like somehow
You always make it purr especially meow

Mermaid

She asked if I was tired of eating mermaid
She did her best on her knees to persuade
Me to take her holes instead she wanted to trade
Places and be my breakfast like my hot mermaid
I watched as she hotly and slowly displayed
Her oral skill as her mouth hotly played
With me dressed as a nurse giving first aid
I make her so hot her body gloriously sprayed
Me with her essence she said I can upgrade
You as she sat on my face and I weighed
My options I had asked for the filthiest
Whore and she took me deep saying fuck your mermaid

Might

She found what I said enticing she said write
Me something about your strength and might
My size and power she loves when I highlight
What really fills her body with delight
Is the thought of perhaps this morning I might
Grab her hair roughly, slipping right
Into her hot holes she's exploding like dynamite
She totally surrenders, there's not any fight
From her as I start slapping, nibbling, I bite
Her neck as I know just how to excite
Her I think I might make her wet, might

More

She's enjoying herself immensely and begs for more
She has no idea the things I have in store
For her as she desires to be treated like a whore
But respected as a person the more
Excited she get the bigger the puddle on the floor
I tell her you are going to lick up your
Juices and rub yourself until it is sore
She couldn't help imagining that I tore
Her dress off and as I continued to adore
Her she got hotter than ever before
She's gagging for it, she wants an encore
She screams what you are doing is working, give me more!

More Pleasure

She replied back baby of course I want more pleasure
I want to touch her in ways that she'll never
Forget how does it get better than her in leather
It gets so hot she's touching herself like you're better
Than anyone else at giving me more pleasure
There's almost nothing greater than feeling like treasure
My desire for her is too deep to measure
I love being why her hands and body meet together
So vigorously if I was your younger professor
Would you do anything for the D, release my pressure
She opened her mouth begging for more pleasure

Morning

She could go for a really good fucking this morning
Something to stop the boredom, the mental snoring
She knew that I could start performing
Cunnilingus getting her ready for warming
She needs it really hot and nasty this morning
Giving her exactly what she craves her yearning
To get really hammered as I start exploring
How to get her to totally forget all the boring
And give her dampness she can't keep ignoring
Her needs she's gagging for it this morning

Naughty

I whispered things to her that made her very naughty
Grabbing her pretty hair and doing her doggy
My hand around her throat so there's no talky
Tying her up makes it especially hot when it's knotty
I'm having her hop on me being so athletic squatty
Now I say open your mouth and be my potty
She couldn't believe I was being so fucking naughty
But she loved it and as I used her body hotly
I take many pictures of her like I'm paparazzi
Leaving her with full pipes her insides are cloggy
I shove her panties in her mouth, she's so soggy
From being deliciously destroyed, she's so naughty

OFFEND

She said let's makeup did I offend
You sweetheart is it possible to mend
The feeling of being compared to other men
Throw my poetry in the trash I penned
So many beautiful things to you and you pretend
That I don't have feelings, that I've sinned
But I know there's no way you could offend
Me forever even when you say you're not my friend
My tears flowing as I think how best to blend
Your coldness with my warmth deep within
Your cruelty towards me, I contend
That I laid my heart open without having to defend
Myself and you say hurtful things, you intend
To create pain so I took the time to extend
An olive branch my art is impossible to offend
I'll forgive you when you hotly bend
Over and show me that delicious rear end

Oh My

There's nothing like when she exclaims oh my
Wait my hands around her neck as I apply
Pressure nothings hotter than looking at her eye
To eye as I take her to heaven at least the sky
Choking her made her a much different hot oh my
Would it be true if I said I know why
You get so heated and leak down your thigh
You enjoy being forced to comply
Force is delicious I love when you start to cry
Out gasping, begging me to use my necktie
And belt bending you over I carefully hogtie
You giving your juices an endless supply

On

She's lying there naked asking if she should put clothes on
Absolutely in your clothes you give me a hardon
Thinking about meeting you for a hot liaison
Your hair looks like you just stepped out of a salon
You're such a goddess, you really got it going on
When you are wearing clothes where do your hands belong
That's right teasing yourself over your thong
You love when I'm filthy, you love doing wrong
I think you're pretty enough for the cover of Cosmopolitan
Legs so muscular looks like you ran a marathon
You're too freaking sexy, go put your clothes on

Part

She said legs are a girl's best friend they may part
She knew exactly what was happening as I start
Warming her up, she's like a priceless work of art
The only thing better than her legs is her heart
She makes eye contact with me as her legs part
She says you're electric, you really jumpstart
My body I know how to make her hands dart
Beneath her clothing, her resolve is coming apart
She loves men with big brains and I'm very smart
I know how to bring out the sweetest, so tart
Is your pie melting let me make you a flowchart
There's a river of pleasure coming from her legs as they part

Personal

She wanted to be my bitch, my own personal
Property I hope her holes are quite durable
I'm going to stick it in your vertical
Smile filling her hot hoes she's an incurable
Slut open your mouth my filthy urinal
I'm going to make it really fucking personal
Dress like my secretary and when you are doing clerical
Work I'm going to remind you how hysterical
You get being my personal bitch the more terrible
I treat you the more that I make the pain unbearable
The most pain makes you wet, filthy animal
Dripping all over your chair like caramel
Taking you in a dark alley having extramarital
Relations you're my dumpster, that's quite personal

Play

I woke up to her asking if I wanted to play
I do in fact so I use my words to convey
That the way you put your body on display
Makes me wake up in more than one way
You whispered won't you please play
With me and I call you gourmet
Taking you in my mouth like a filet
Throwing you around roughly, you love horseplay
I woke up so horny dreaming of you today
Thinking of the best way to portray
My desires use your hand to start to play

Playfully

I know how to delight her by acting playfully
Do things that excite her by acting bravely
She enjoys her breasts being played with painfully
Right now she's feeling so sweet and savory
Making her experience things by tastefully
Being sweet and spicy playfully
Imagine I come over for some sugar, all neighborly
Ripping your dress off, acting so brazenly
I start warming her buns like a bakery
Grabbing her by the hair, teasing her anally
I leave my desire all over her facially
She licks her lips and fingers gratefully
Would you like more and more I ask playfully

Please

She needs it so fucking badly she begs please
Make me absolutely dripping between my knees
Make my legs shake and my hips start to seize
She's getting heated while I blow on it the cool breeze
Makes her feel so much pleasure as I please
Her mind and body my tongue sops and I freeze
Right there I'm unlocking her safe with my keys
She desires the sexiest, naughtiest sleaze
Expertly I continue to playfully tease
Her making her body raise temperature several degrees
She loves when I roughly start to squeeze
Her naughty as she's begging for more, pretty please

Pleasing

She said that she really wanted me to start pleasing
Her so I started lifting and squeezing
Her throat that makes her start heavily breathing
Firm slaps and my hands provide sensational teasing
I'm in her mind which makes her hands start pleasing
Herself once again the more I continued beating
The more she cried out from joy my hand meeting
Her ass makes her start shaking and screaming
She loved it rough and she's receiving
The beast inside she's careful to start greeting
Me properly as her desires keep increasing
I make her very hot, which she finds most pleasing

Priceless

She said invaluable but I hope she means priceless
Building her up, making her feel success
Bringing her joy, reliving her stress
The more I ask may I continue to bless
You the more I make you a hot mess
Polite men that speak bravely are priceless
I want to give you pleasure to excess
Also to make you start leaking through your dress
It blows up and reveals the most beautiful, priceless
Butt I want you thinking of me as you press
Your magic button, I'm making you hot yes
You love being treated lovingly as I caress
Your mind in such a sweet manners, my process
Is to meet your unspoken needs do I express
Myself in ways that feel unusual, like priceless

Professionally

She asked a question, do you write professionally
I think that I do, I hope that it makes you exceptionally
Hot when I use my mind to give you heavenly
Sensations am I warming you up professionally
When you think of me I hope you're pleasantly
Surprised by how I increase the temperature steadily
I want you to know that I think of you preciously
Bringing delight to you is my ultimate delicacy
You excited my mind and body so readily
Let my tongue feel so hot and velvety
Am I turning you on most professionally?

Prove

There's nothing that I'm trying to prove
It's about your cheap, whoreish groove
Being called trashy really gets you in the mood
You're so nasty but your body will move
Its hands to grab yourself easy to prove
That the cruelty towards you will improve
Your days for money you're happy to remove
Your clothes cheap trashy whore loves me being rude
Take my dick deep down your throat you'd
Love how I pinch your nose to prove
To you that being nasty is your favorite food
If you quit resisting I know you would approve
Of being gagged the stickiness is easy to prove

Punishing

She had a fantasy that I really started punishing
Her it's making her drip the puddle is becoming
So big and her juices keep running
Down her leg she's never experienced such cumming
She got so heated the more I started punishing
Her and it really made her plumbing
Very damp she's reading this and rubbing
It so fast she needs more, she needs it so fucking
Bad she's on top of me and dry humping
My leg like a bitch in heat I'm running
My hands through her hair and unbuttoning
Her blouse soon there will be more punishing

Pussy Suck

After a long, firm massage came time for pussy suck
I'm licking and sucking like I'm earning a buck
For ever time I make her shake like she's thunderstruck
She's been longing for the hottest pussy suck
Well tonight my dear you are in luck
I want you to back it up and you're ready as fuck
For my tongue to leave you completely awestruck
I found her most sensitive chords and struck
Them repeatedly then it's like my mouth is stuck
On her pussy, everlasting pussy suck

Puzzling

I enjoy playing puzzles with her, what's puzzling
Is how my words make her start becoming
Such a hot mess her desires begin bubbling
Out when I carefully and slowly start running
My hands over her body, her pleasure is doubling
Bigger and bigger pleasure puddles how puzzling
I give the the hottest smacks all encompassing
Pleasure she loves when I start roughing
Up her breasts she gets so hot from the suffering
She loves being tied up, she enjoys struggling
To capture all of me she's warmly guzzling
All my dick down her throat she's functioning
As my hot wet hole, she starts hotly sucking
Me where'd it go, it disappeared, how puzzling

QUESTION

At this hour she loves to answer a kinky question
Has anyone like a florist been able to freshen
Your flower with grace and ease able to lessen
Your stress while licking your hot midsection
I've got a million thoughts, but only one question
If I was a priest and it was time for your confession
Would you talk about your nastiest indiscretion
Talk about how you swallowed it all, your digestion
Of your own juices has become an obsession
I know you spend all day touching yourself another session
Dreaming of a hot, steamy, rough lesson
Makes your nipples erect and your face redden
If you are here than who's in heaven
That my dear is a rhetorical question

Real

She asked about my naughtiest fantasy to make real
I like most when you're able to feel
Beyond sexy, goddess like the way I steal
Your attention and the inner whore you reveal
Is that you're the nastiest slut, like for real
Each time you do something sexier you peel
Another layer off your depravity I appeal
To your freakish parts using my tongue with zeal
Imagine you're reading your dms as I kneel
In between your legs, tone like steel
I bring it out of you, no use trying to conceal
That you need it really bad so the ideal
Thing to do is open your legs wide, for real

Record

She felt her desires growing and hit record
I speak to her frankly, she loves how forward
I'm being the way that I speak hotly towards
Her revs her engine, gets her so floored
She felt so naughty when I released her stored
Up passion and she adjusts the camera hitting record
She's moaning and groaning as I've struck a chord
Just perfectly with my words I hotly explore
Her desire to be a lady but her inner whore
Wants me to slam her against the headboard
Act like you're late on rent and I'm your landlord
Tying you up with my extension chord
Here comes what you've been craving, hit record

Release

She really needed something to release
Her sensual side and I provided the grease
Giving her pleasure that never would cease
Touching her center, she's my centerpiece
I fill her with joy and peace
By licking every crevice, every crease
With my tongue I slowly increase
Her pleasure making her hot between the sheets
She said I'm devilishly good and a sexual beast
She needed more pleasure, she needed release

Resist

She asked what on a woman's body can't I resist
I'll answer your question, roughly start to twist
Your nipples using your hands and wrist
When I I think of your favorite part one does exist
It's that inner whore you can never resist
The opportunity to hotly play with your tits
Your longings grow as my tempting words persist
There's too many of your favorite parts to list
Your talented tongue gives me a deep kiss
Then your tongue goes in my ass I wished
For the naughtiest, nastiest hole as you mist
Me with your juices I've got a bowl no drop missed
Your hot, flowing essence is impossible to resist

Ripped

When I found her alone I quickly ripped
Her clothes off she's eager and well equipped
To be used like a piece of meat, she loves when I hit
Her and grab her roughly by the hip
She loves when I push it in between her lips
Being made to take it, having her insides ripped
Open make her begin to uncontrollably drip
She loves being forced, she's a force addict
Nothing else made her hornier she stripped
Down but I said get dressed so I can rip
Off your clothing then I easily flipped
Her over smacking her and started to spit
On her face which made her happily
Lick it all up she puts her fingers deep, she dipped
Her fingers in as ordered, she loves when I'm strict
Almost as much as when I surprisingly ripped

Ripping

She was wearing a robe this morning and getting
Very playful so I suggested long, hot licking
I start playing rough and she starts grinning
I forcefully take what I want I'm ripping
Off her robe and her panties are sticking
To her body my breakfast is warm and she's sitting
On my face as I quickly start spinning
She loves when I'm forceful, it gets her dripping
The harder I use her body for delicious sinning
The more she enjoys as I keep ripping
Into her hotness I savor her juices I'm sipping
Her best tasting parts, she continues glistening
When I use my large hands to roughly start gripping
Her hair as I smack her I'm really ripping
Into her ass she loves it and starts wiggling
Pleasure puddles develop as her legs keep kicking
It gets her so hot the way I'm physically and mentally ripping

Romance

She was feeling ready for some superior romance
The effect of my words get her in a trance
Her hands start working overtime there's a chance
That I'm going to make her leak through her pants
She wanted steamy, gripping, passionate romance
I'm her favorite fertilizer I make her plants
Bloom and watering them is easy when she grants
Me access to get her more steamy with fire romance

Romantic and Nice

She enjoys when I'm very romantic and nice
She needed to hear it, she needed it twice
As good as anything else before so can I entice
Her to feel amazing as I feed her an orange slice
I know that genuine admiration is her ultimate vice
Something started happening the more romantic and nice
I get with her it touches her in a very precise
Manner if she was a flower she'd be birds of paradise
When she's cold I want to be the fire to her ice
Helping take her pleasures to new heights
Which is exactly what happens when I'm romantic and nice

Rougher

The harder I hit you, the rougher
I am to you the more I discover
How nasty you are a true freak undercover
When I grab your hair and start to smother
Your face it makes you melt like rubber
I'm punishing very firmly, then I get rougher
It makes you leak, there's no use in trying to cover
Your desires there is no other
Thing you desire then to be crushed, I'm your crusher
I know how badly you enjoy it when you suffer
Taping your mouth shut now there's a stunner
Putting a remote vibrator inside yourself I've got the buzzer
More pain my owner, you beg for a rough lover
Which makes me happy as I continue to get rougher

Sketching

This beautiful goddess said I was really good at sketching
I told her back well you're extremely fetching
I enjoy when she slowly starts stretching
Opening her tone legs she's hotly spreading
Whispering draw me like one of your French girls get sketching
Touching herself so vigorously, ripping her leggings
I'm in between your legs and heading
To heaven giving you something to start getting
Very heated about I'm in your lap checking
Your temperature seems your appetite isn't the only thing I'm whetting
When you think of me I hope it makes you start begging
For more pleasure, please sir keep wetting
My panties and make me another sketching

Skirt

She was going shopping for a new skirt
She asked what kind I like and I blurt
Out when I see your legs I get so alert
She's trying on many for me and I start to hurt
She really excites me showing off her skirt
I am very polite but also a huge pervert
When it comes to legs you look like you exert
A lot of effort into doing your best to divert
My attention the way you tease in your skirt
I can see how excited you are through your shirt
My favorite skirt is the one which you insert
Your beautiful body into, I love your tight skirt
Especially when you start to insert
Your fingers making yourself rapidly squirt

Smiling Dose

She was having a rough day so I gave her a smiling dose
When she's struggling it's very easy to diagnose
The difference between feeling great and gross
Is if you lie back and start to close
Your eyes my tongue will give you another smiling dose
I know what makes you smile the most
Playing your piano hitting all the high notes
If I make you melt like butter and spread on toast
My tongue knows how to make you overdose
On pleasure pleasing you with an extended smiling dose

SNACK

I'm sneaking into her bed for a late night snack
She loves when I invade her senses that's a fact
She found it irresistible naughty mixed with tact
She bent over and begged me for a smack
She was drenched with desire that snack
Is very wet it looks like you'd like me to attack
Your firm, muscular body has anyone told you that
You're the whole buffet, not just a snack
Cute perky top, but my attention falls on your crack
You love hot, heavy breastplay I know the exact
Spot on you to grab tightly with no slack
Your greedy mouth trying to fit my whole ballsack
In your mouth my warm nuts are your favorite snack
With those legs that look like you ran track
Into your mind, hotly I'm able to hack
Your desires you are riding me like on a racetrack
You're a thoroughbred, making a hot soundtrack
Of you gagging, drooling, spitting, inhaling your snack

So

She hotly said I made her really wet, so
Much hotness her pussy could melt snow
She's touching herself hotly down below
As she enjoys the river starting to flow
She bent over and gave me a good show
It excites my mind very much so
I want to make her shoot like a star and glow
The effect of genuine appreciation whispering slow
And steady spicy mixed with sweet, a great combo
She bent over in my face whispering hello
To my kitty, you've made it so wet please sow
Your seed inside me her naughty little photo
Is very hot, like the rest of her beauty, it's so
Fucking delicious I want to taste her rainbow

Sowing

I believe in reaping what I'm sowing
If you say you love someone start showing
That thinking of them makes blessings start overflowing
When I think of you my spirit starts glowing
Thinking of you makes me exceptionally outgoing
You sunk my battleship now I'm just rowing
In a sea of blessings when the waves start throwing
Me around I think of reaping what I'm sowing
In turbulent atmospheres I start slowing
My focus exclusively on the most mind-blowing
Outcome imaginable having certainty and knowing
That making it looks easy requires an easygoing
Nature no shit no roses and I'm growing
Beautiful things as I am reaping what I'm sowing

Special

She felt quite wonderful when I made her feel special
Helping her experience joy at a different level
When I think about her best angle there are several
Things to share about her, she's so special
She's one percent angel and ninety-nine percent devil
I like warming her and finding her disheveled
She treats her body like a temple, a beautiful vessel
I cuddle her and don't put her on a pedestal
Let me hold you in my arms embracing you in warm special

Squeeze

Her lap is getting hot and she starts to squeeze
Her clit it is getting so hot as I tease
I'm rushing over her body like a cool breeze
Making her want to be a good girl she said please
Make it so engorged and easy to squeeze
Her hand is moving fast and she starts to freeze
She's going up and down on her personal trampoline
Using my tongue to slowly do the ABCs
I want you to imagine me in between your knees
As your legs grip my head, you're starting to squeeze

Squirting Doll

She's a really nasty, slutty, squirting doll
She desires to be made to crawl
Thrown like a tiny thing against the wall
I like making her squeak which is all
She can do is moan and be a squirting doll
When she walks by I make a catcall
Calling for her pussy she can't help but fall
Down to her knees such a useful squirting doll
She slowly starts licking each one of my balls
I'm taking her shopping at Northpark mall
She's got a very fancy and expensive haul
She earned it roughly, by being a leaking squirting doll

STEAK

She begged me for my meat, give me your steak
Which she would soon learn was a huge mistake
I hit her repeatedly and she started to shake
I'm making her body tremble like an earthquake
My pulverizing her like a piece of steak
She likes the way I smack her cake
How I am just nasty and never fake
Anything I want you to imagine I wake
You up and use you like a fucking rake
You can't do it to the willing I'm happy to rape
Your senses my hot little piece of steak

Steaming

She's like a locomotive, I'm making her steaming
She never knew it could get this hot is she dreaming
The effect of my words gets her totally beaming
I'm making her think the dirtiest things as I'm cleaning
Her inner thighs with my tongue, carefully teasing
Her and she pushes me head into her lap demanding eating
I'm making her so hot, liquid rushes out, she's steaming
I'm making pleasure puddles everywhere she's leaking
So much there's a river, she's streaming
From all the teasing I've got her teeming
With hot desires she starts slowly leaning
Back letting me soak my face in her steaming

Stray

There's a certain type of woman I'd never stray
From, there is a particular way
That I express myself I hope that I may
Reach your heart, hopefully I can convey
That you deserve a man that doesn't stray
You're very refined and beautiful in a classic way
Such lovely hands and nails you display
Dear you are my definition of gourmet
It's probably been too long since you received a bouquet
Of flowers you're a petite sophisticate, a filet
Mignon and you are sizzling like the sun's ray
A woman of your caliber deserves to not have anyone stray

Studying

The she sat, diligently studying
I slowly started treating her like a pony brushing
Her beautiful hair and my fingers start running
Down her body as my touch makes her start shuddering
I'm nibbling and licking as her nipples start puffing
She really found it quite hard to focus on studying
I massage her sculpted legs and she's becoming
Very relaxed she's ready for me to start stuffing
Something in her pretty mouth she's loving
How thoughtful I am, and she starts blushing
My hands and words get her desires gushing
I take my time with my mouth I'm not rushing
She finds it fun to study wearing nothing
But a smile as I'm in her lap attentively studying

Taking

I dreamt of you, you were taking
A shower and you whispered am I making
You excited as I said dear you're breathtaking
You started moaning replying it's so stimulating
The effect of my words on your body is fascinating
I'm taking you to the edge, I'm taking
You in the shower you've been craving
Something really hot, something titillating
When you read this you can't help placing
Your hand right there, your body is shaking
As you read the saucy things I'm creating
How easily you surrender to my persuading
You love getting excited and start taking
Photos of all the wetness as you enjoy my vibrating

Talent

When it comes to being warm I have talent
I think of how best to get you in touch with your pent
Up desires when you know time has been spent
On focusing on your pleasure all problems went
Away I'm a magician of pleasure but my talent
Gets better when you smile and I can smell your scent
I now know the fragrance of heavenly sent
Thinking of your excitement helps me invent
New ways of doing things you dreamt
Of opening your package, enjoying your present
When it comes to delighting you I'll never relent
If you enjoy my words my tongue has even more talent

Talking

She said she was ready for some late night talking
Meaning she wanted me to make it hard for her to be walking
The next day ripping her dress and her stockings
Doing things so naughty, beyond shocking
She really enjoyed my unique way of talking
She's reading this and her hips start rocking
I'm invading her senses, totally stalking
Her desires as her hands and breasts are interlocking
She's squeezing her breasts during late night talking

Taste Drive

I'm enjoying her juices taking a taste drive
The harder I hit her the more alive
She feels I'm so rough she might not survive
I'll choke you really hard and then revive
You with my dick have a taste drive
I'm going to shove my whole fist, all five
Fingers in your hole when you arrive
You drop to your knees and start to dive
For my lap hungry animal you know I've
Never met someone that really will strive
To be my personal cumbucket I strive
To hurt you more than anyone giving you a taste drive

Teaching

She knew a lot about desire, but I started teaching
Her a whole different level, giving new meaning
To hunger she suggests I start feeding
The animal inside her, her passions are screaming
I just learned that when I keep exceeding
Her wildest dreams it makes her desire rough breeding
I think she'd bring her whip and ask me to start beating
Her bottom just the thought makes her start leaking
She says I must know your method so I'm proceeding
To tantalize her in new ways her desires are wreaking
Such havoc I want her mentally creaming
All over her legs if there's something worth dreaming
About it is a filthy student worth teaching

Team

She asked if I wanted to be on her team
I said perhaps, what will be our theme
Can our team name be Team Obscene
When you're in any outfit you cause a huge scene
Especially when we can all see the stream
Leaking down your leg right in between
Your legs I love seeing your luscious cream
When you bend over I stare at the stream
Coming from you I'm glad I'm on your team
I'm hoping your shorts split at the seam
You're doing your best to fulfill my dream
I'm putting thoughts in your head, none of them clean
In between your legs is hotter that a sunbeam
I'm playing with fire, I'm on your team

Thought

When it comes to pleasure I put a lot of thought
Into what will get you absolutely hot
When you're heated and I see a drop
Falling down you leg it really got
Me motivated it's time someone taught
You what discipline means you thought
You were composed but my words effect you a lot
My little doll tries her best to squat
On me and her body and mind fought
With everything it had but the thought
Of me spanking you made you get caught
Misbehaving touching yourself as I tie a knot
Bound, gagged, submission can't be bought
You desire to be the nastiest, you desire to be taught
Now being punished is your only thought

Thoughts

She could sense I was having dirty thoughts
About her she makes my dick leak lots
I dreamt I tied her tightly with knots
She loved playing secretary, she said boss
You're staring at me again are your thoughts
About tossing me around please toss
Me like a doll as she made eye contact and uncrossed
Her legs she said give me your special sauce
She's working overtime to totally exhaust
Me and when she bent over her panties were lost
She wiggled her ass asking having any dirty thoughts

Thread

She was so turned on, every single thread
Was damp and I know how to giver really good head
Rushes making her swear and her face turn red
She's touching herself furiously in her bed
I'm a dirty, dirty vulgar man and instead
Of fighting it I know exactly how I led
Your hands into your panties you slowly read
Each word imagining yourself there as you shed
More clothing until your panties hang on by only a thread
Good little girl has no idea what's coming up ahead
You're getting so crazy, your legs hotly spread
You're a hungry, filthy thing, I keep you well fed
I love it when I'm able to drench every single thread

Tomato

I smacked her ass repeatedly until it was as red as a tomato
I whipped her ass and watched how clow
She started leaking and I increased the flow
By hitting her harder each whack, just one blow
Makes her body as red as a tomato
I spit in her face and called her a nasty ho
Which turned her on the places we'll go
Will be filthy and I'll make your body glow
With pleasure as I know how to excite you below
Spank, spank, spank your ass looks like a tomato

Too

She asked me to also shove my fingers in her mouth too
She loves how small she felt when I easily threw
Her against the wall and her eyes quickly grew
As I made her face sticky as fuck with my glue
I know exactly what gets her boiling she's into
Freaky, nasty, dirty, playing so am I too
I'd like to make you black and blue
Tomorrow you are soaking your panties through
Your dress, the things I call you
Like filthy fuckmeat, cumdumpster, whore are all true
Right from your ass I'm in your throat you blew
Me so well it made me start to stick my shoe
Inside your hole running a train choo choo
All of my friends get to make use of you too

Trash

She was an absolute dumpster, real trash
Using my big hands to firmly mash
Her tits as I kick her violently I smash
Her body as she leaks from her hot gash
You're the trashiest bitch ever trash
Hitting her so hard she gets whiplash
I use the metal part of my belt, the brass
Hurts her and marks her body and makes her splash
She's so nasty, disgusting, such a piece of trash
I stick my foot in her hole and she starts to thrash
I'm putting her body to good use as I bash
Her pretty face spitting all over the trash

True

She had a very wet dream she wanted me to make true
I'm nibbling her neck, waking her up a few
Things you should know that I know what you
Really need put on your highest heels and do
You like when it leaks down your leg, to your shoe
I break her boredom with the most refreshing new
Ideas she needs mental stimulation, it's true
I'm getting her hot like a volcano so she'll spew
All over me she enjoys that I'm so into
Female pleasure, I'm like the morning dew
I refresh her flower with moisture anew
I get her insides wound up like a corkscrew
Giving her great dampness helps renew
Her spirits, she's getting really wet, it's true

Twisted

She suggested we play Twister, I do like her twisted
I'm thinking of a game that keeps you interested
Beyond curious I suggest we play lifted
Lifted is a game that I just recently invented
I bet it gets your panties in a knot, so twisted
I'm going to make you grateful that you listed
Out all your desires because I'm quite gifted
She could tell I meant business and shifted
In her seat as I watched slowly as her hands drifted
She said I never do this but you have resisted
My advances and no man has ever assisted
Me as well as you do in getting me so horny and twisted

Very Special

She was endearing whispering you've very special
She opened up to me fully as my vessel
I filled her with desires on a different level
I'm no angel and she's a dirty devil
Her longing to please me is very special
She jumps on my lamp and tries to wrestle
My pants off as I laugh and we revel
I hold her tight and she purrs as we nestle
Together our warmth together is very special

Whole

You make my body ignite I mean my whole
Being if we were roleplaying your role
Would be quite simple, be my wet hole
I want to use your beautiful face as my blowhole
I think you'd enjoy surrendering control
Would you trust me to use your whole
Body for my pleasure I'll make you stroll
Down to my office like you are on parole
You really need this job as I Stick it in your butthole
I'm in so deep I'm drenching your soul
You're going to have one simple goal
Lick it all up, do what you're told
Every single drop you swallow hole

WRITE

She found herself so excited reading as I write
To honor her and bring her the most light
She lights up like Christmas and I love to excite
Her soul, her mind, her body deserve endless delight
I'm imagining being inside her, she's so tight
The best thing to motivate me when I write
Is knowing that I give her an appetite
For sensations that make her spirit take flight
I hope when she's experiencing a lonely night
That she dreams of being there like I'm right
There stroking you sweetly, you can't help but to bite
Your lip when you read how vulnerably I write

Yeah Fuck

She said fuck yeah and I was like yeah fuck
Me you keep my hands permanently stuck
On my dick as you open your mouth awestruck
She's playing with her pussy again and I struck
Her favorite horny spot right there yeah fuck
She wants to be hit like a dump truck
Dump my load on her she starts to go buck
Wild playing with her pussy she sneakily tucks
Her panties in my pocket whispering yeah fuck
Fucking fill them with your red hot spunk
She opens her mouth, to her knees she sunk
She says you're so stinking nasty like a skunk
Making her holes hotter again yeah fuck

Younger

I started teaching erotic writing and though I was younger
Then most of my students I was filled with wonder
When I saw that my student cut a hole in her jumper
I looked closely and could see a cucumber
Sticking out of her maybe it's funner
If I back up and explain I found panties on my bumper
With a note attached containing a number
It said I'd let you stick it in with no rubber
I felt something touching me, something was under
My desk and it was her, she said I love them younger
Her muscular legs were smothering my face her hunger
Was making her body rumble like thunder
She's pushing my head firmly trying to smother
Me with her juices and I got a glass to have another
Drink of it later she was hotter than summer
It gets her so heated seducing another man that is younger

www.ingramcontent.com/pod-product-compliance
Lightning Source LLC
Chambersburg PA
CBHW070541080426
42453CB00029B/803